BY MOON AND SUN

By moon and sun

WALTER PERRIE

"*Intellege te alium mundum esse in parvo, et esse intra te Solem, esse Lunam, esse etiam stellas.*"

ORIGEN

(*Understand then that you are a second world in miniature, and that the sun and moon are within you, as are the stars.*)

Edinburgh
CANONGATE
1980

Publisher (small)

First published by Canongate Publishing Ltd
17 Jeffrey Street, Edinburgh EH1 1DR

© Walter Perrie

ISBN 0 903937 91 3

The publishers acknowledge the financial
assistance of the Scottish Arts Council
in the publication of this book

Designed by James Hutcheson and Ruari McLean

Set in Imprint and printed and bound
by W M Bett Ltd of Tillicoultry

9520
(16·4·91)
C

Wyr sindt der metall anfang vnd erste natur/
Die kunst macht durch vns die höchste tinctur.
Keyn brunn noch wasser ist meyn gleych/
Jch mach gesund arm vnd reych.
Vnd bin doch jtzund gyftig vnd dötlich.

Succus

Preface

It would be unreasonable of me to expect readers to be familiar with all those sources which have moved me or which have caught my imagination and which are therefore the proper raw material of my work. Consequently, I have appended some notes to this text; notes which I hope will suggest the associations which certain images hold for me, as well as providing fragments of information perhaps not readily come by.

I expect those readers who are familiar with the techniques of twentieth-century poetry to feel at home in parts of this work and to be puzzled by other parts. Modern poetry is characterised by its introspection. That self concern is a response to the horrors of our century. The miseries witnessed by our age have left us deeply suspicious of those who command fine phrases and large armies, display generous feelings whilst continuing to exploit the feelings of others. Ours is the age of the professional hypocrite and of his public acceptance. Small wonder then that modern poetry is reticent about feeling and hesitant about language. At the same time, it is sometimes difficult to distinguish an excess of reticence and hesitation from quiescent cowardice.

The techniques of poetry are not means-to-ends but are the fabric of the poet's enterprise and the relation between the way language is used in a poem and the way in which it is used in daily discourse says as much as the supposedly translatable contents of a poem. The point has been elaborated with some elegance by Marcuse; "Analytic philosophy often spreads the atmosphere of denunciation by committee. The intellectual is called on the carpet. What do you mean when you say . . .? Don't you conceal something? You talk a language which is suspect. You don't talk like the rest of us, like the man in the street, but rather like a foreigner who does not belong here. We have to cut you down to size, expose your tricks, purge you. We shall teach you to say what you have in mind, to 'come clean', to 'put your cards on the table'. Of course, we do not impose on you and your freedom of thought and speech; you may think as you like. But once you speak, you have to communicate your thoughts to us – in our language or in yours. Certainly, you may speak your own language, but it must be translatable, and it will be translated. You may speak poetry – that is all right. We love poetry. But we want to understand your poetry, and we can do so only if we can interpret your symbols, metaphors and images in terms of ordinary language.

The poet might answer that indeed he wants his poetry to be understandable and understood (that is why he writes it), but if what he says could be said in terms of ordinary language he would probably have done so in the first place. He might say; Understanding of my poetry presupposes the collapse and invalidation of precisely that universe of discourse and behaviour into which you want to translate it. My language can be learned like any other language (in point of fact, it is also your own language), then it will appear that my symbols, metaphors, etc, are NOT symbols, metaphors, etc but mean exactly what they say. Your tolerance is deceptive. In reserving for me a specal niche of meaning and significance, you grant me exemption from sanity and reason, but in my view the madhouse is somewhere else."– just so. And on the precise location of the madhouse, Marcuse again; "In this society, the rational rather than the irrational becomes the most effective vehicle of mystification." for, in this society, rationality has become a synonym for a rationale of domination, manipulation and exploitation. To that rationale there is but one sane response; the Great Refusal. André Gide has said it better than I could; "Comrade, do not accept the life that is offered you by men. Never cease to be convinced that life might be better – your own and others'; not a future life that might console us for the present one and help us to accept its misery, but this one of ours. Do not accept. As soon as you begin to understand that it is not God but man who is responsible for nearly all the ills of life, from that moment you will no longer resign yourself to bearing them. Do not sacrifice to idols.''

If the wickedness which the present order embodies must be refused, then that, like every refusal, is an implicit acceptance of the negation of that which is refused. Prior to the Great War, poetry in English was written mainly in an intensified or heightened 'ordinary' language; ordinary in as much as it maintained and asserted continuous, rational narration as a basic technique. The refusal of that continuousness by Pound, Eliot and others asserted the disruption of a hitherto ordered universe; a disruption which shunted Eliot into the only siding available to him – religious orthodoxy with all its attendant retrospections and quiescences – and Pound into a home-made fascist aestheticism.

In the West, capitalism has deprived poets of a social role. Their audience has been restricted to friends and a few enthusiasts. Consequently, the most realistic expectation which a poet can have is that through his work he may heal himself. But since poets, like other men, are social products, without a social healing the poet must remain infected by the condition of his time. In some past societies the healing function was performed through the rituals and public actings out of religious ritual, myth and dream.

The language of dream, with its unlimited lexicon of image, situation, gesture and utterance, is capable of a discourse continually multivalent, fluid and ambiguous. It relates to our experience in a quite different way than do the languages of the sciences, logic and reportage. The latter seek to avoid ambiguity and to operate within the limits of the highly restricted functional aims of their respective language games. Myth and some kinds of poetry use language in such a way that it partakes of some of the characteristics of dream-language and of science-language.

In the interpretation of a dream, a particular image or utterance may be understood as sustaining at one and the same time mutually exclusive interpretations. As in the dream, so in life. A named object, like a dream image, subsists within

ix

a vastly complex web of relations. The languages of science attempt to cope with this complexity by piecemeal description. Having had their lexical elements selected in part on the basis of the exclusion of ambiguity, they are, outwith their own spheres of application, inadequate to the expression of those elements in our experience which we do find ambiguous. It is in precisely this area that art excels.

The attribution of significance to an utterance, thought or action is always relative to the perspective and interests of an interpreter. Scientists, with the support of some philosophers, have sometimes alleged that the sciences are free of any such bias. History, considered as the totality of past events, necessarily eludes us except insofar as we are its product. Given the equal reality of all phenomena, then any one event is caused by the totality of prior events. All written history resolves this dilemma by adopting theories of 'significant cause'. Since all sciences are interest laden, history is not excluded on that basis from its claim to be a science. In fine, there are no 'soft' sciences and if we consider history to be the study of those interests which have given rise to the different perspectives both of the so-called 'hard' sciences and of most written history, then, as Gramsci has noted, history has a good claim to be the science of sciences.

The languages of art are subject to the same strictures as those we have noted with reference to the languages of history, the sciences and daily discourse. In this regard the distinction between fantasy as private imagination and imagination as public fantasy is a useful one. As Iris Murdoch has suggested, those would-be art works which fail to translate the contents of subjectivity into publicly accessible materials fail to become art and remain products of fantasy. If we recognise that all views as to the nature of reality are partial, then those views are products of public fantasy, that is, they have an imaginative content, albeit that content is restricted by the necessities of praxis. Politics is the attempt to reconcile reality as it presents itself to us with how we should prefer reality to be. Those preferences are constituted by an imaginative (public) translation of fantasy accreting on private sensation. Freud and Marcuse formulated the conflict in terms of that between the Reality and Pleasure Principles. Inasmuch as art attempts such a reconciliation, we may properly call art an aspect of politics – and vice versa – and account for a number of difficulties which have puzzled aestheticians. It seems probable that the flow of subjectivity; conscious thought, fantasy and dream, originates in a biological mechanism generated as an adaptive response to the thwarting of an individual's desires by his situation in the world.

A poem is autonomous in relation to its author and yet relates in an intelligible way both to his situation in the world and to his subjectivity. Like politics or the scientific theory, a poem effects a mediating relation (a healing, reconciliation) in the conflict between the world-as-given and as desired. A poem achieves its mediating function by synthesising those conflicts or oppositions in a form which is both public and private. A poem therefore cannot be explained formalistically any more than the functions of a computer can be explained solely in terms of its hardware. Successful art, like successful politics, heals. Part of the tragedy of our century is that so little art and so little politics can be accounted successful.

Passionelle to Jonathan

*"The Lord shall cause thee to be smitten before thine enemies;
thou shalt go out one way against them, and flee seven ways
before them; and shalt be removed unto all the kingdoms of the
earth. And thy carcase shall be meat unto all fowls of the air,
and unto the beasts of the earth, and no man shall fray them
away."*

Deuteronomy

"They make a desert and they call it peace."

Tacitus
(attributed to Calgacus)

Delicate eyelids
          offer to sleep
                    blue-veined
their marble
          of the night's satieties.

You were
          so beautiful that day.
Your lips and eyelids
               dried my mouth
                         without warning
and I remember
               nothing now
                    I said.

Red-gold
          the tongues of hungry trees
                              lick
at the thin, autumnal dawn.

I

In April the Autumn
                    seemed
                              long distant
as a lifetime
          gone.

The city
        at the window
                      stirs.

Cité, cité
          swarming city
                        thick with torments
                        thick with dreams
you do not fear
                the insubstantial ones
the standing stones
in Heraclitus' stream
                    nor love.

No Jonathan
          lies dreaming by you
                              in the hills.

Perhaps you did love
                    and have sought
too long
        the white buck in the thicket
                                      of despair
the artless one
whose measured song
                  is dew on the wilderness
at dawn.

Cité, cité
          carcase in the desert
                              air.

2

Absurdities!
The night retracts
                its promises
of dream and reverie.

Ritual warily
            we strutted out
            our peacock movements
                            gold, blue, green
slow ceremonial
            prefiguring
                        the inebrieties
                        and the rending
dawn.

Mistress my moon
                slips
                    one pale rim above her coverlet.
The stars dim out
                caught up
                        in our diaspora.

Out of Canaan
                into this
                        diaspora
nor any homecoming
                    for you or I.

Close up
            those brindled, grey-green eyes
and say
            goodbye to Canaan
                        Canaan of the desert eagles
and the songs.

3

Jonathan, the songs
                    depart without farewells
and every day
             the city
                  swells its acrid dissonance
and the journey grows
                more arduous
terrain
        more treacherous
                  the desert
                      blooms profane
illusions of fecundity
while we
        together
            have grown weary
                weary traversing dust and
                          rock
rutted by the tumbril wheels
        the cannon wheels
        the tracks of tanks
                the myriad
desert myrmidons.

And the journey is
                for a shadow's sake
                      occluded light
behind us or before
            shadow
                the desert sun accentuates.
Ice
   breath of the desert
                dawn
chills
   the fever-breeding flesh
chills
   the starry knots of space
                  in glacial
passionate day.

4

I have fed the flame
                with hazel boughs
cut from the white-buck thicket
                                cut rowan also
                        and the apple bough
but found no staff
                the twinning vipers twine
and fear
        the desert eagle
                        feasts on carrion
again.

Flamelight
            and the eagle's eyes
                            have opened.
Flamelight
            shadows in ochre corners
deep-socketed eyes
                more deeply.

Shall we escape
                shoe-click on cobbles
and you
        be breathless beside me?

A moon-pale track
                between
                        the two sharp rocks
                between Bozez and Seneh
feet slithering
            where rock is
                        treacherous.

Thin fabric
            sticking to our backs

Are we pursued?
        Not yet
        but soon
            so quickly
                on.

Grey before sunrise
            the unaccustomed liberty
and fabric chill
        on breast, back, shoulders.

Behind us
        eagles prowl the night
high over
        Shannon and the Somme
                awash with carrion.

Pale flesh
      resilient
          defies the dawn
renews
     night's promises
returns
     the inebrieties.

Among the insubstantial ones
              triad and quaternity
twinning vipers twine
         about the pole
staff of eternity
        where nothing
           satirises
              nothing
till boils break out
        on the Old King's face
and, lacking purity
        the kingship's lost.

Mistress my moon
               creeps on
                    her cyclops way.
I tilt to her
          unclouded eye
                 my cornucopia
kaleidescope of images
                blues and purples
                gold, grey, green
profusion
        past all
             mere fecundity.

All this unreal
           unearthly beauty
                a painted cone
                and a mirror or two.

Or lingers yet
          beyond the grasp
                 of prying fingers
poking
pulling things apart
            some sign
                unguessed at
even yet?

All the painted images
             pale
peacock and eagle
          pale to this
             perplexity
and all I can do is
          withdraw
nod
   to Satanael or God
            and say
            No thanks, your go.
            You shake the fucking thing
            You shake up
the kaleidescope.

Truth like the heroes
                has departed.
All the little lies
                come true.

We have breathed too long
                        the desert air
and have not found where
                anywhere
                        Jonathan
                                the low salt pools
                                the twilit shore
where herons feed
                stirring the stars
                                in vortices
of quiet concentration
                fishing
                        for Sirius and Betelgeuse.

Herons mate in the blue-grey hills.
We know only
                desert eagles
red-eyed
                eagle of the skulls
red-eyed
                eagle of the dripping beak.

Suffer me
        to kiss thy lips
                        O Jonathan.

Blue, blue
        the baleful
                wild forget-me-not
gallows garland
kingly garland
                Jonathan.

8

Thickens and rises
        smoke
              as the yew sap hisses.
Courage
     and the clear lines are
           obscured.

Now let us praise our noble dead
Iain Lom and Owen Roe
          for want
          of better things to do.

Keppoch
     stands before the onslaught.
The old
     stand firm.
The young
      must flee
         to a new beginning
             or defeat.

Who could
       chose exile with the Earls.
Those who remain
      can only wait.

And so   I wait.
But willingly?
      No, nor welcoming.
             It is un-natural
to welcome them
      their cold, clear lips
the insubstantial ones.

9

The noble Earls
           have taken ship
                      O'Donnell
                      and the great O'Neill
and I
      not of that company
      nor with Montrose at Inverlochy
      nor waded
              breast-high
                    to the flood
                          at Limerick.

Many's the great O'Neill
                has fallen
since I saw you
          yesterday
              Owen Roe, Owen Roe.

Many's the one I praised
                  for courage or beauty
is gone into shadow.

Many's the eagle
          the ditch has taken
Owen Roe O'Neill.

And so   I wait.
For us
      there is no swift return
                  among our kinsmen
                  and our ancestors.

Rain runnels
          stone.
Durable convictions
            seem less durable.

To rain perhaps
            to water we return
                        not dust
but wading
            breast-high to the flood.

Perch' io non spero
            because I
                        cannot turn again.

Did Villon choose
            the gibbet then
or Dante, exile
Yeats the water-weary bitterness
                        of rage in Sligo
Pound, the cage?

Take ship?   To where?
What better
            than to wait
                        in poverty and eloquence
with smiling Jonathan
                        for friend?

Fill up the flesh
            with history
                philosophy
                        for neither
man nor woman
                can assuage this
                        long captivity.

Perch' io non spero.
No waiting ships now, Ezra
                  no keel
to set to the breakers.
Not Odysseus, Ezra
             that journey was
                       to victory
                       through victories.

The journey is
             no longer to
                  but from.

Limerick town is burning down.
What shall we do
             with all the dead?

Defeat
         hones down the ages
                   to a cutting edge.

Lay out the coffins in a cross
now that the world is
                ending?

Litter the earth
           the bones of heroes
bones of unheroic men.
The silver cup is
            sold or broken
Keppoch's praising
             and lamenting
                     desert air
consumes them
         all.

They tell me that they'll soon
                              be farming deer
on Morvern and on Mull
                         green Mull
                                    of the MacLeans.

Green
       grey-green and brindled eyes
dare not endure
                   the desert
                              light.

Green
       blue-green and white
                             the whirling sphere
dares not endure
                   but circles
                         circles to the sun.

Moons rise up
                on endless worlds.
Lovers
        issue gentle out.

Green
       grey-green your eyes
                              in dust and empires
springing from the tears of men.

Sebastian
           sea-bastion
                         androgyne image
only
     a little longer.

Green
      light
            green and gold
                  the flights endure
one crimson drop
            on pale, fine skin
your hair loose back
                  eyes closed
tight against
            the ravages.

What, pluck the arrows out?
Anoint the wound
                  for other martyrdoms?

Dissolution and coagulation
is the nature of
            the art
                  and ritual
                        the final state
the incorruptible
            androgyny.

Larksong
      wells in the azure air.
Hawthorn
      reaches slender stems
                  towards the sun

What unbreaking dialectic
                  breaks us
                        from that
singing throat
            the measured
                  dark
                        impalpable
in an unceasing
            passionelle?

Nota bene: In arte noſtri magiſterij nihil eſt Secretum celatũ à Philoſophis excepto ſecreto artis, quod artis non licet cuiquam reuelare, quod ſi fieret ille ma lediceretur, & indignationem domini incur‡ reret, &apoplexia moreretur. ☩Quare om‡ nis error in arte exiſtit, ex eo, quod debitam

C ij

Creation

"The final mystery is oneself. When one has weighed the sun in
the balance, and measured the steps of the moon, and mapped
the seven heavens, star by star, there still remains oneself. Who
can calculate the orbit of his own soul?"
Oscar Wilde

"Zion shall be redeemed
  by justice."
Isaiah

"What is love? revolt
  against a world that is
  in favour of a world to be.
  an act of insurrection,
  death and resurrection.
Richard Livermore

It is on the mountain
                    grief begins
                              grief like an agate
rainbow banded rock
                    girdling the heart
                              agate
my birthstone.

And Schiehallion
                    rising from our centre is
                              a wilderness
the ascent
          always in that giant shadow
backpack filled

with shards of promises
and uncut dreams
                              collected on the way.

Always obstructions
                    bramble thickets
                    tangles
                    snags among the undergrowth
and higher up
          the rockfalls
                    body-breaking crags
                              and cold
for all that I wrap well
                    in malice and anger
drawing my self-coloured coat
                              close about me
never certain
          whether the ascent is flight
                              or search
                              or merely is.

Close by me
          on the shadowed moor
                              a solitary hare
erect
     sniffs at the setting sun.

Black-tipped his ears
                    track subtle stirrings on the air
alert
     to distant footfall of a deer
nearby
     a goldfinch' whirring wings.

Above the hare a falcon
                    hovers
answering the shifting wind
                    in twisting bursts

seipsis secundum equalitatē inspissentur. Solus
enim calor tēperatus est humiditatis inspissatiuus
et mixtionis perfectiuus, et non super excedens.
Nā generatiões et procreationes rerū naturaliū
habent solū fieri per tēperatissimū calorē et equa
lē, vti est solus simus equinus humidus et calidus.

D

that hold him
       stationary
           to his prey.

A baying drifts up from below
               continuous.
Tsvetayeva, I smell the pine cones
                  in your lucid air.
Tsvetayeva, the evening breeze
                brings other mountains
rising
      monstrous through my brain
Ben Dorain and Jehovah-Jireh
Cuilin, Sinai
        and your un-named slopes
               all thronging in.

And you, dark prince
        come stalking also
             generous huntsman
supple as light through the bracken
           quiet and cunning.

Four ways the wind blows
          over the bones of Schiehallion
and the evening star
        cold candleflame
           no solace
in these northern parts

Come prince
       call up your stallion wind
saddle and mount up
         swinging South
           spurring on
until he set us down
       to play

                        among gay, watered gardens
bright with olive
                fig and vine
                        where we may walk
the heady woods of juniper, bay
                cypress, pine
                                and lemon blossom
celebrated by the dancing bees.

Their music
                low as a throbbing kettledrum
                among their emeralds and incense is
the loom
                whereon they hum
                                instinctively
their bright brocade
                        swift shuttles through the warp
between
                the dumb polarities
                        of light and shade.

Here stands a king in chariot
                                bearing a sickle
                                and the books of law.
Here in temple robes
                you wait
                        long patient
                        in the humid dark
and here a hunting scene
                        the pack a-hue upon the hare
and here a court
                a mountain dawn
                        a dreaming man.

Four ways the wind blows
                        over the bones of this
mountain
        inhospitable to fig or vine.

21

Sweet prince, remember me
                          and be my guide
across the moor
                to that dark apex on the dawn
your tongue
              caressing at the root
                                      of things
to bring to burgeoning
                        long dormant seed
bright harebells
furled bracken tips
                    and scatter Springtime
in my wintered North.

You, my lord
              who flank me keenly
                                    in the tender dark
be tentative
              instinctively
                            the baying pack
may scent our spoor
                    and rend
                              sweet fibres
of the sportive hare.

Out of the bruise-blue
                        broken sky
                                    the evening breeze
blows from the South
                      continuous.

In the South now
                  it is Winter also
                                      rain, mud, wind.

In the beginning
                  when they gave us bread
they threw it at us

                    from the backs of trucks.
In Winter
            mud is everywhere
                            even in the tents.
When the wind blows
                    sand gets in the food.
Sometimes the wind
                is very strong
                            and the guy-ropes break.

They say
        we have forgotten our homeland.
When I was young
                I wondered why
I had no homeland
            of my own.
                        Now I know
it is better to fight
                to liberate our homeland
for ourselves.
            No one else will.

We did not always live here
                        where the hills are
                        ochre and eroded
but they drove us out
                with only our name
                            into the hills.

They say
        they have a sacred right.
It is not true.
                Fragile as birches
                the poplars here
                        are bare and white.
It is the wind
            Sirocco
                desert wind.

23

Jerusalem, the evening breeze
                            brings pine scent
and the sound of bells
                    out of your dreaming
darknesses.

Jerusalem, tonight I am
                        a violin
                                to all your songs.
City, how did your wells run dry
                your markets empty
                and the evening breeze become
the only pilgrim
                to the Holy Mount?

Tonight
        I shall not forget you
                            city of returns
but flow through you
                    an evening breeze
                    a pilgrim
to your ancient wells
    your empty markets
        anguished walls.

Tonight
        I shall be played for you
                            and be
a crown of song
            for you
                    whose name burns on my lips
a seraph's kiss.

Over the golden Dome of Omar
                            bells
sound from the Holy Mount.
I am become
            a violin

24

and you
           a stony-hearted whore
have been no more than
           a name
for whom the olive trees
           of many gardens
                  have been felled.
For your sake
           many vinyards have been levelled
                  and I
least of your children
           must sing true
               tonight.
Jerusalem, I am become
           your song.

But Jonathan
           what if I'm driven
               mad by Spring-wild
burgeoning
        to blossom into
            folie de grandeur
                what then?
Why then
       I'll write
           as March hares do
           upon the grass
           my tracks
             exposed to predatory view.

A cruel business
           being mad I mean
               a trial
                 deadly too
must give me pause
         lest you
           should whistle up the dogs

25

you judges, jurymen
you rack and pinion
                specialists in trial
                        by ordeal.

And if at bay
            I should confess
                should have wrung from me
who he is
            his secret
                    name
would that infernal baying end?

He is a falcon   and an eagle
he is a roebuck   in the thicket
he is a hound   shall rend the hare
he is the sting   of a viper
and the cure
            he is a blood-red
                    death-white
                    seed-black man
of the sky-blue harebells
                    carpet Schiehallion
in a Summer dawn.

He is a light   my mother's son
he is a shadow   across the dawn
he is a rampant cock   a tree
a night-black stallion   riding me.
His name is
            Jonathan
                a child of Israel.

26

Into a barbed perimeter
               O Israel
you have driven your victories.
With Phantoms, Skyhawks
                 over Tyre
you have blazed a yellow star
                    to pin to the shirts
of your victories.
In Sinai and Jerusalem
                 you have buried their bones.

In silent trains
           from Germany
your victories come seeking you.
From Poland, France
               from the Ukraine
               from Czechoslovakia and Hungary
your quiet ghosts come
               silent shadows
                    lovers, mothers
                    children's ghosts
                    come
begging on their hands and knees
                 whimpering
out of the night to you
             O Israel
               in Palestine.

Hast heard the death cry
             of a hare
               come tendril
up the mountain
          grave?

The telling, Jonathan
           the tale must rend us
woundable as hares.

Quiet as hares then
                    sly and swift
                            be
evanescent, shifting and symbolical
                                    the truth
                                    untellable
                                    entire
and tell of travels
                    to and from
                            desire.

Who made me
            my rainbow coat
                        all poppies, dogs
                        hares, hawks
                                    and eyes
a host of open eyes?

Whence its colours
                    my gay coat?
Who wove it
        dyed it
        gave it me?

Jonathan wove me
                my gay coat
                            texture varied as the dyes
now silk, now hessian.

His blues
        harebells picked at dawn
    reds
        the eyes of tired men
    greens
        of bracken
                        ghostly greys
    yellows
        honey from Schiehallion's bees

black
      hair of a princely boy
              all woven
to innumerable shades
           no simple speech encompasses.

Your eyes excite me, Jonathan
no less than
        cock, lips
        hands or hair
           still hazel
              wells
deep-set desire.

From deep-set wells
        from groundwater
           spring
all our moments
      of longevity.

Well-water, wave-swell
        tumbled stream
            commingle
in our riding frame
      to weep
        to fertilise
          to bleed
salt song and bitter
      in our northern wine.

And shall we bleed, weep, seed
          enough
to wear Schiehallion's ramparts down
         build
water-polished stone on stone
        despite that gravity of law
pulls every human structure
      down?

corrūpitur, neqȝ ex imperfecto penitus fecundũ artem aliquid fieri poteſt. Ratio eſt quia ars prī mas difpoſitiones inducere non poteſt, ſed lapis noſter eſt res media inter perfecta & imperfecta corpora, & quod natura ipſa incepit hoc per ar tem ad perfectionẽ deducitur. Si in ipſo Mercu rio operari inceperis vbi natura reliquit imper⸗ fectum, inuenies in eo perfectionẽ et gaudebis.

Perfectum non alteratur, ſed corrumpitur. Sed imperfectum bene alteratur, ergo corrup⸗ tio vnius eſt generatio alterius.

Speculum

30

Let you and I
              defy all gravity
                           save gaiety
stripping our ragments
                       of malice and anger
journeying naked
                  lightfooted, freely.

The telling, Jonathan
                      the tale
be swift
         your tongue on mine
                              as deer at gallop
on high-brackened moor
                        or bees
                        at gold-tongued heather mouths
until our kiss ferment
                       its heady liquor
         flesh secrete
                        its honeyed wine.

In the beginning
                 so it begins
ours is a drinking song
                        measureless wine
in the cup of the void
                       sweet and the bitter wine
mingling together
                  deep without eddy.

In the beginning
                 so it ends
ours is a love song
                    striking discord through the deep
and time the Muzzein
                     calls us to our new devotions
                                measured motions
restless through these

                    city bars
                            longing to be
measureless again.

Light up the bars!
The dark outside is
                    mournful
                            deep.

In Rose St and the Canongate
where weary barmen watch the clocks
one by one, the bars close up
                            bright finches
caught in gin-trap laws.

Law, law again!
Mourn ye drinking men
                    O mourn
                            and bare your heads
let pass the cortège
                    of our howffs
                            their undrunk spirits
                            their untasted wines

Below the public bar
                    dark prince
                            unseen
your hands caress
till like some permanently stupid fish
                            to bait I rise
and you cry
            Home!

Four ways the wind blows
                    over the bones of this
city of the half-desires
                    un-numbered, hushed velleities.

City, like a bow
                across your bones
                                the crazy wind
plays crazy tunes.

City
     your mad dancers we
                      go reeling home
the roads unchosen
                but the steps
                        our own.

Past brazen shops.
Their lidless glare
                outstares the dawn
                        the bars all closed
your creatures passing
                hurriedly
                      in overcoats
and buttoned poise
                embarrassed by our clasp of hands
our drunken joys.

On George the Fourth
                we are subdued.
Along the High St
             laughter dies
                  below foreboding
black St Giles'

Here in the heart
             between the black cathedral
                  and the courts
a North wind blows
             where cobblestones are
glistening crowns
            of sunken skulls a-peep
from shuddering deeps below

33

                              black, polished crowns
the street lamps gem
                    with topaz grief
                                   and ruby pain.

This street is high
                  this Royal Mile
                                 rising on its pile
of bones.

Over the Bridges
               down we go.
By Salisbury
            Schiehallion rises
                             where Orion was
and for the Plough
                  a starry skull.

From George St and from Princes St
I hear the baying pack.
Over Queen St and Leith Walk
I see the patient hawk.

In Leith
        no sky-blue harebells bloom
nor sportive hare
                 salutes the sun.
In Pilton and Craigmillar
                         red-eyed
working men each day
                    forfeit their ecstacy
                                         hour by hour.

On George the Fourth
and on Dean Bridge
                  we walk among the kissing dead
self-coloured coats
                   drawn tightly on

34

                                    while far below
the muttering ghosts
                    grow rancorous.

City, city
            so much loved
                            precarious our balance is
between Schiehallion
                    and the damned.

Sweet prince, by candle light
                            let's love
unless the street lamp should betray
                                too harshly
tears for sunderings
        for seed and shooting stars
                                all dimmed
                                diminished
our inheritance to this
                    one bar, one star
                    two seedling tears
of muddy waters
    fiery airs.

Your body
            so intensely by me
                            nestling in the night's black fur
whinneys to the touch of love.

Like fishermen
                caught in a little boat
                                on a rising tide
our senses quicken
                no word spoken
                                but the struggle's on
for shoreward
                nerves
                    wide open.

35

Swells and falls
       the riptide sea
           Sirius
uncannily brilliant
        overhead whirrs
            hawklike
on the whirling sky
        and writhing, prince
             you cry again
as starseed
      shoots the firmament
           the waters of heaven
parting from earth
       and darkness
          from light.

The terrors of love's making done
          the quivering
and mortal skin
       quiesces to the tides of sleep
one palm spread flat
        across my belly
            breast pressed tight
against my back
       swelling, falling
          quiet, calm.

Sing me a sea-song, Jonathan
         sad for our sunderings
never returnings
       heartwrecks
on the storming tides
        the rock-pierced hulls
        the broken masts
        the cargoes spoiled.

ROSARIVM
ANIMÆ EXTRACTIO VEL
imprægnatio

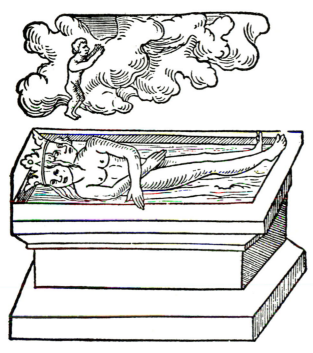

Hye teylen sich die vier element/
Aus dem leyb scheydt sich die sele behendt.

De

The passionate candle, Jonathan
                          is soon consumed.
Rigid bone nor supple sinew
blood nor tears
                  nor shooting seed
                              run swift enough
none swift
          as the quick
                      untrammelled light.

The dog star
            throbs to his zenith
                          and the city
seems sleeping
              dreaming over
                          its intolerable dead.

Darkness and light in my city
                          random
                                  fragmentary beauty
memory traces
              on your strings of light
                              George Square
          its lilacs all in bloom
                          and cherry blossom on the Meadows
          where we have been
                        between
                              late May and early June
          and seen
              a flock of finches
                          swirl
          about the bright boughs' filigree
                              gold, yellow, green
          wheeling
                  turning azure air
          on blurring wings

38

                weaving
                        on their timeless space
                                        nets
of their ageless ritual
instinctively
                curve sines
                        hyperbolas and arcs
                                        carve
multilinear complexity
                        in silence on the azure air.

The finches weave
                for ever
                        in and out.

Our sunderings
                alone
                        are timed
                                our only drinking hours
confined.

Our love star in her window
                        pales and cool the garden
summons us
                desirable to rise to
                                from too trammelled passions
of our bed
                while on the limes
                                the finches weave
their daily burden
                in and out.

Mortal city
                sounds coil up
                        milkfloats, busses
                        taking men to work.
The black road states
                its sanity.

One hand rests on my shoulder
                cool
                      a finger traces
down my spine
          your urgency behind me
                    hard
but harder still
      to find
             unfolded by the light
your shadow and my own
                once you and I
now absent light
          accusing us
             of history.

So hard this dawn
           unkind to come so chill
on all the hot extinctions
        of our night.

How can I weigh these
          patient ghosts
              sweet prince
as you weigh me
         in scales dextrous and sinister
your shadow
      lover
        fished from some archaic order
you whom I can never weigh
            elusive one
whom no fish-hook nor lure
draws from your glittering deep?

Out of darkness I have come
          to be
           a tongue between your lips
a terrified naming
a protest of love

                    an unfinished creature
stumble-fumbling over
                    words
                          of an elusive song
its summons
                    enthralling-eluding me always
stranded on this
                    northern summit.

Sometimes, Jonathan
                    your weight oppresses me.
You know I am no Atlas
                          nor heroic Naoise
                                    and unbearable
you at my back
                    until your hands touch mine
and the burden
                    eases
                          seems less wearisome
and bearable
                    a little longer.

Below
          along the latticed streets
                          light seeps
through loveliness and grief.

From Arthur's Seat
                    to the Castle Rock
a North wind weeps
                    its grey lament
has bared its head
                    and weeping
fled the cortège of the city
                    lights
                          where all the shadows are
my own.

41

Below
     between the two sharp rocks
on crown-emblazoned Palace gates
           a red-eyed eagle rouses
waits.

Hard by the talon-guarded gates
          I fell
and falling cried
       his name
           cascading corpse-lights
down each street
      cold fingers
          to pry rooms apart
and darkness
      down each artery.

Shall I escape
      shoe-click on cobbles
          and you be
breathless behind me
       thin fabric
         sticking to my back?

Take flight?   To where?
Only the empty Castle gapes
      where all I fled from
gather where
     I named them
      naming found them
      naming bound them
        ground them to ash
blows on the wind
      when the flames have died
          dear enemies.

Onto my shirt you pin
      on star

PHILOSOPHORVM.
CONCEPTIO SEV PVTRE
factio

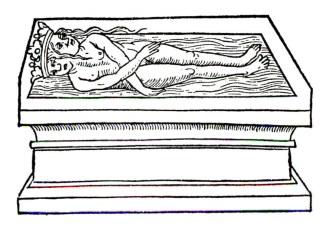

Hye ligen könig vnd königin dot/
Die sele scheydt sich mit grosser not.

ARISTOTELES REX ET
Philosophus.

Nunquam vidi aliquod animatum crescere
sine putrefactione, nisi autem fiat putris
dum inuanum erit opus alchimicum.

                              for all my victories
and shave my head
                and make me walk
                              my crowded mile
to flinch at every rictal smile
                          a city whore
                              collaborator
for a few dry rags
                of sanity.

Hands reach
                to shred my tattered coat
                              of dowdy lies
and frailty
            and hang a placard
                      round my neck.

Not remains
            but to endure
                      surrender.

Take flight?   To where?
What's left to dare
                  when ghosts come home
to claim their own?

Flamelight
            ochre
                lights the hills
                        fanned furnace bright
by Northern gales
                and in the sleepless dream
                                  I turn
to you
            whose eyes are mirrors
                        smoking of my fierce disgrace.

44

PHILOSOPHORVM

ANIMÆ IVBILATIO SEV
Ortus seu Sublimatio.

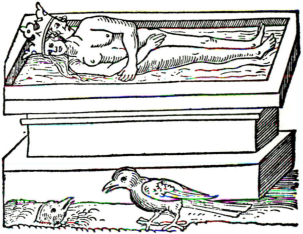

Hie schwingt sich die sele hernidder/
Vnd erquickt den gereinigten leychnam wider-

L iij

45

Dark prince, sweet executioner
                              whose life is one death
and whose death another
                  death in life
                              come claim your due
dear hawk
            above this hare
                        come stoop
                                    and read

your shadow on the moor
                        the legend that I bear
your name
            read
                  He Who Did Not Love
                  Enough
                              runs with the pack
                              flies with the hawk
to walk among
            his kissing dead.

Dear prince
            no court nor punishment
                              can cure
                                    nor yet deter
the many failures
            of my heart
                        each little death
and so   I wait
                  fast in the shackles
of a shackled heart.

And from a coign of this
                  high rock I hear
a stallion's hooves come
                  drumming thunder
                              down the dawn
and on his back

                    with Jonathan
                            I ride out
on my reckoning
                    down my red road
                                the city blazing
furious rainbow
                    of my birthstone.

Ash and smoke
                    my city now
                                dispersing on the heart's chill
air.

And your voice, Jonathan
                    soars up
                                an eagle on the hills
and cries
            Streets and domes
            flow from you now.
            Cities all
            are silt and sand
            the river carries
            to the sea.

Up and on
            the stallion rises.
City, sea
        and mountain
                    pale.
                The earth candesces to
a candle flame
            blue-white
                    diminishing
                                before the sun.

Innumerable stars entwine
                    in coil on coil
                                of serpent light

47

writing before me
                red and gold
                          its filigree
across the void.

And your voice, Jonathan
                cries out
                      All this flows
                      from you now
                      all this
                          and turn
take hand in hand
kiss tongue to tongue
                to comfort me
                      across the whirling
multiverse.

And still the stallion
                treads the deep.
Slowly
      the glittering beast
                coils up
                      to one pale circle
seed
    closed tight against
                the still
                    immensity
and your voice, Jonathan
                cries in this cup

        I am your island
        you, my broken-masted ship.
        On my shore
        from its storming tides
        your craft may find
        its land again
        home-havening to be
        safe-moored to me

dark rock
no furnace melts nor sun
nor frost may rive
nor rains erode
endurable through all
this loss.

My roots embrace
the crystal
of the mountain's core
and from my ramparts
on the dawn
the dreaming stars
are thrown.

In all this
multiversal dark
no hope
if you cast off
from me.

The seed
        unclenches
                to a sapling tree.
Root and branch
        spread their hands
                out into the void
and in my heart
        the deep dark pales
                to deepest blue
hares stand alert
goldfinches whirr
                and in cathedral coolness we
below its leafage lie
            intwined
            inseparably
            sans thou
                or I.

49

FERMENTATIO.

Hye wird Sol aber verschlossen
Vnd mit Mercurio philosophorum vbergossen.

Look, Jonathan
                the coiling East
where colours of the coming dawn
                                stain all the edges
of the opal dome
                vermillion, claret
                amber, gold
                            and strokes of emerald
on pearl.

See how these colours
                        well
                            from fissures
of the Eastern rim
                    light after dark
                                    the miracle
                                    of miracles.

Silent, slowly
            so our sun emerges
                                from its seas of man
cascading light
                the first light of creation
on your face and limbs.

Most lovely scion of our love is
                                light
                                    transfixing you
to radiance
            my hard, my black
            my dark-haired Cuilin
                                of the night.

Slowly, silently
                I turn to touch
                                your hand
responsive to my own
                        and lingering

                                        kiss tongue to tongue
before we go
                among what images must coil us on
to night again.

Into your harbour, love
                I sail
                        between your lips
to reconcile
            the rising and the setting suns
the bright processions
                    days that utter us
                                from dawn to dawn.

We are their tongue
                time's protest
                        to eternity.

So
    together we must out
                    on city streets again
to walk among
            our kissing dead.

City, city
            causeways, chasms
                    on your court's wrought iron gates
are Scotland's emblematic beasts
                            lion rampant
                            and a unicorn
                            below a crown.

What crown is this?
Set with what stones?
On whose head
shall it rest
            at last?

The dreaming beasts
              by city courts
                         incongruous.

What, Edinburgh
            still the same
                   in such a dawn?
Sometimes, city, it has seemed
                    if someone cried
in Scotland now
            Aux Armes!
            Aux barricades!
he'd only find
         you have no French.

Comme un miroir
ton pauvre coeur
est brisé
sur l'étage d'amour
mais comme un rêve
d'éspoir qui dure
s'élève un image
de ton âme
si pur, si pur.

Below the Bridges
             where the traffic brawls
the tide still rolls
           surf rancorous
                 and in its utterance
Skyhawks are droning over Tyre
                  while round us
restaurants and massage salons
               purvey
their customary joys.

At eight in the morning we're off to our work
Hurrah, Hurrah,
and when we get home we're shagged as a Turk
Hurrah, Hurrah.
For poets and painters we don't give a toss,
their ivory towers are a dead bloody loss
and we'll all be sports and join in the fun of the fair.

But some of them can't seem to leave us alone
Hurrah, Hurrah,
complaining and moaning and spoiling our fun
Hurrah, Hurrah,
so shoot all the commies and lock up the queers,
make democracy safe for at least twenty years
and we'll all be sports and join in the fun of the fair.

The fair and the circus are coming to town
Hurrah, Hurrah,
we'll oggle and goggle and laugh at the clown
Hurrah, Hurrah,
we'll swing on the swings and shy at the stalls
and try to forget that they're selling our balls
and we'll all be sports and join in the fun of the fair.

We'll helter and skelter and dodgem about
Hurrah, Hurrah,
the chamber of horrors we couldn't miss out
Hurrah, Hurrah,
we'll shriek and we'll giggle and add to the din
and – try – to
        forget
           we're
              as
                ugly
                  as
                    sin
and we'll all be sports and join in the fun of the fair.

From alleyways and sad cafes
                        the children come
to join the fun
                guaranteed in running order
from the pack
and from the hawk
                to scale the body-breaking crags
and bear
            each scar and bruise
            each thorn and rock.

By moon and sun
                the children run
                                about the pitfalls
                                    rockfalls
                                    snags
grow sly
        and swift and ultra-wise
                                in realistic compromise.

Coiled about this
                city's core
                            lidless eyes
glare at the light
                from desert sand the dawn has stained
a bloody red.

Violence will come
                    time and again
so long as men
                are pinioned
                            on the racks
                                        of loveless capital.

No man is free
                until all men are
                                free to love
and if this

                gay compassion
                        is insane
                                why then, I'm mad
                                and would be mad again.

And so   I wait
                        no longer lost
in cowardice or inactivity.

To you, dark rock
                I moor this craft
                                come storm
                                come executioner.

We will not be panting does
                        hound-apprehensive
through the bramble thickets
                        on Schiehallion's moor
but, if we must
                at bay at last
                        turn
                                you and I
high-headed stag
                before whose fury
all the pack withdraws
                        or venturing too close
are slashed, impaled
                on the rending antlers
                                of our love.

At Karameh
                when they crossed the Jordan
Skyhawks, tanks, artillery
                        twelve hours we fought
as though grown rooted.
                We did not retreat
                                one step.

No war is over
           till this battle's won
when love and justice
                arm in arm
                       come limping home.

Ended, the struggle ended?
It has hardly begun
                cascading from the eastern rim
each dawn.

Words!
      Wild
           whirling birds again.
The poet-whore plays
                sly affection at a glance
will sell himself
           to any casual man
stand up erect
        on any podium
                unless
                      he love.

So all the poetry
            comes down to love
thence to a silence
thence to a
           merciful oblivion to city songs
the dog-star howls
           to music of your lone guitar.

Children of longing
           betrayed and betrayers
where will you run to
                from unloving streets
when your ghosts come
              home to claim their own
and every bridge

each cobble stone
leads straight down
into the abyss?

Sell all you own! It's not enough.
Immune your ghosts
to any bribe.

Children of longing
where will you hide
when in George St
and Charlotte Square
the falcon hovers
and you hear the hare?

Where will you put your ghosts
when they come
on invisible trains
you cannot derail?

In what cell
in what office index
file them away
when Tsvetayeva comes
and kisses you
full on the mouth
and you taste how it was
on the mountain
ashes and gall?

Will you take your ghosts
on guided tours
of aerodromes, shipyards, factories
smile
when they tell you
this wheel cost
two hearts
for this engine
one soul?

58

Will you send them a telex or telegram
                              saying
        DON'T COME
petition the courts
                for an order restraining
                              and stating
        By Order, Desist
                        from seditious desires?

Will you call out police or the army
                              to stop them?
American bombers
                will not fly for you then
rifles not shoot
napalm not flame for you
                        to whom love is
invasion and manipulation
domination, exploitation
occupation and possession
purges, trials by ordeal.

Children of longing
                no tablets will help you to sleep
through the morning
                        they come to the doors
                              of your bedrooms
in Morningside, Duddingston
    Craigmillar, Liberton
                        when no-one's to blame
and the world finally leaves you
                              alone
knowing it's you they have come for.

When cafes and pubs
                        finally close
                              where will you poise
not to see the abyss
                and Schiehallion

59

                    monstrous before you
and all the bright multiverse
               passing away?

When ash and gall
               are in your mouth
dreams and delusions
               burning about you
who will caress you
               unravellers
                    of the delicate nets
creation has woven?

Look, even your hands forget you.
How proud they have become
               your lonely hands
dextrous and sinister
               demented shredders of the dawn
shredding and selling
               hares and harebells
               poppies and men
               products, commodities
               objects for markets.

Children, come morning
               who'll mourn you
by gravestones for ever
               erect?

Shadows nor machines
               have tears to shed for you
who shatter a world
               on the racks of your willing
                    your terrors
                    your law
                    your controlling.

When you run
                as a hare from the coursing
streams will not hide you
                        who still all their love-songs
to water-plants, water fleas
dragonflies, kingfishers
otters and water-voles
algae and lilies.

No sea will shelter you
nor darkness shield you
                who curse it
nor forest will
                throw down its branches
                        to aid you.

Even the stars cannot hide you
the multiverse
                not deep enough
                        betrayers of brothers
by brothers betrayed.

At ending then
                when husbands and wives
                        have deserted you
seek out your children
                you made them
                        abandon their ecstasy.
They will destroy you
                at ending.

Children, where the earth has gathered
                        in forgotten crevices
sow harebells
plant saplings of elegant birches
plant rowan and poppy
                for finchfruit and beesong
and shelter for lovers.

Their tenderness and guile
                    alone
are god enough
            to blossom
                    blue and crimson dawn.

Jonathan, between us now
                    be nothing
                            saving sounds of love
to ride
        high on your eagle back
                        to ecstasy
we may not abdicate.

Now let us to our poppied earth
                        our crimson blooms
incongruous
            on northern moor
                        to trample out
                                our loving space
where heather
            shall forgive our weight
        frond-fingered fern
                    unclench for us
high on our marvellous miracle
                        mountain
                            in the lucid air.

Frailty alone
            may win your confidence
                        sly, shy one
in Schiehallion's dawn.

Only those who claim
                no lordship
                        over deer nor eagle
                        bee nor man

nor any living-dying thing
     that loves and leaves
the earth again
    may come to know you
       crooked bear
sleeping Winter-long
     till Spring comes burgeoning.

Love thaws
   the fruitful river
     of the eye
to flow in that complex simplicity
      of every natural thing
until the eye itself become
     a living mirror
      to the sun
reflecting hawk and hare
    as one.

Viper, eagle, harebell, poppy
falcon, deer and dreaming man
     each one image
in the mountain's dream
     flowing sap of the twining tree
twists roots through all
    diversity.

Sweet prince, my thought turns now
      towards that other prince
not Jonathan
nor Denmark's son
    but him
     who from the shore
at Loch nan Uamh
    with Lochiel
     took ship for exile
promising return
    and on this

                    desolation
                              our inheritance.

Often in despair I thought
that every gentle, brave
                    or generous thing
                              fled Scotland
from that graven shore
                    for France and Rome
                              to sink
into defeat's debauch.

That loyalty and love
                    had gone
that loyalty of love
                    rooted Clan Donald to the spot
in fearful pride
                    as the Butcher's shrapnel
scythed them down
                    that crazy, lovely loyalty
rooted endurance
                    in its very grief
                              to blossom
bloodbright
          from Schiehallion's topmost pinnacle
a miracle
          before a faithless world.

Tears thaw some truth.
In love's grief
                    generations weep
for though the days
                    on Scotland since
have come as dogs upon the hare
                              and though, dead Prince
your order was another slavery
                              remained to you
some semblance of a human form.

No worth in you
                    but in that
                              love
                                   you drew about your cause
fine, multicoloured cloak
                         about a corpse
as every tyranny
                 has drawn on love
                                    as Spartans once
tied lover's arm
   to lover's arm
                  to run together
                                  on the spears and swords
or beardless boys
                  crazy as stallions in Berlin
reared blood and bone
                      on armoured metal
                                         from corrupted love.

Your loss
         our harsher, swifter degradation
in the tenements
                 mills, pits, factories
where men must sell
                    their beauty
                                 for another's gain.

Though you, dead Prince
                        did not return
but left great Cluny
                     eight years in his cage
awaiting you
             an other, nobler prince
                                      has come
not to Glenfinnan and the clans
but to the shops and factories
                               to backlands

of our stone perversities
                    he
                        who spoke swift thunder
to dear John MacLean
                    who gave
to one from Raasay
                    generous spirit
                    fiery tongue
                            speech hard and bright
as rowan berries
                    red and gold
                            in Gaelic's Autumn
for the tokens
        of his love.

And to a postman's son from Langholm
gave the breath of life itself
                        his speech
a glorious, pure, clear bell
                    ringing from Whalsay
and Montrose and Biggar.
In their unshackled loyalties of love
                        the bitter ghosts
are stilled
        and with them comes
                        a new rebellion.

Battle is already fierce
                    not for the soul of Scotland only
but for all
        our Palestines
                    guerilla war
for every office, slum or factory
                        where man claims lordship
over man
        where property takes precedence
        where capital would measure love
        or law enslave
        or fear deprave.

Not one Palestine
                but all
                      the homelands
                                that we are
ourselves.

The ascent will be steep
                    long, arduous
                            in shadow
and the broken promises
                      weigh heavier with every step
struggling always to maintain
                        our bond
                                ideas and actions
bound together
                arm to arm
                    by thongs
of critical self-scrutiny
                      continuously questioning
our attitudes
              towards our comrades
              and the mass of men.

The uncut dream is not enough.
The task to understand
                      and work to transubstantiate
ourselves
            all facets of a crystal
                      world made whole
with hand and eye
                and name.

The struggle is life
                    multiversal crystal
of the mountain's core.

Modes of production, distribution
              oppressive structures states establish

forms of law, religion, ethics
                education, science, art
all facets of a single gem
                        each change of light
on any surface
                shimmering dimly through the whole
each lighting all
                in a continuous
                        mutual transformation.

The artist's role
                to see
                        as far into that crystal as he can
not only to illuminate
                our past
nor even to articulate
                our future
                        but a total revolution
in his life
                so that by living
                        he create that future
                        which fulfills our past
that limit
                to which art aspires
                        impossible apex
where Schiehallion
                penetrates the sky
and by the intense light
                of sensual experience
to see both future and the past
                        as one unbroken crystal
mountain
                indivisible
                        unbreaking
                                dialectic of the light
that has been
                light that is
                        and is to be.

Hope is not vanity.
Like a long awaited Summer thunderstorm
the revolution in humanity
                              will come
in large, slow drops at first
                              gradually quickening
its rush of rain on foliage
                              to a muted sobbing
on the vibrant air
                    until, exhausted of its grief
the patient planet
                stills.

Then, when you think it's ended
                              suddenly
the shackled heart of heaven
                              opens
drenching
          your senses in warm blood
gushing
        from the world's wounds
splashing
          breast-high
                      on the pavements
lightning
          forking from the massed, black clouds
thunder
        beating frenzied drums
                              until your griefs
cascade like rain
                  heart lifting
                              unexpectedly
and like a violin
                  you are become
                              its song
till that intensity
                  of power and grandeur

PHILOSOPHORVM

ABLVTIO VEL
Mundificatio

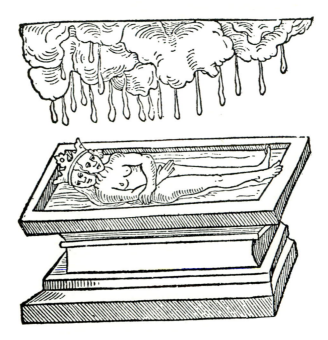

Hie felt der Tauw von Himmel herab/
Vnnd wascht den schwartzen leyb im grab ab.

K iij

70

                                        leaves us
silent
humbled
awed.

Then, from a blue-grey
                        breaking sky
                                        the sun
emerges from its dark
and all the senseless rages and divisions of our past
are seen in that white radiance
                        of love.

From all our heartlands
tenements and high-rise flats
shops, office blocks and housing schemes
from Dundee, Edinburgh, Aberdeen
Glasgow's anguish, the tormented West
                                        a voice will rise
and be
        a violin
                to all life's songs
                        cascading
on the morning breeze
                        its airs of pilgrimage
unceasing
                on the Holy Mount.

And to our wintered North
                        a southern wind
                                will bring
harebells and poppies
                of our love's shy frailties
and girdle
        blue and crimson Spring
about Schiehallion's naked stone.

And in intenser light than this
                    our shadows
seeming darker still
                    that love irradiate Schiehallion
till our sacred planet
                    luminescing to its keener light
quickens and pulses
                    heartlike
                              or a living kettledrum
nerves wide open
                    light and sound and motion
arcing
          over time and space
                    love-rituals
                              of lambent grace
instinctively
              and root and branch
                    reach hands
into the deep
              quick black
                    and the shuddering heart
of Being pales
          to deepest blue
                    in a dawn
of untellable ecstasy.

Dear prince, no promise
                    can redeem what has been
nor any dawn annul
                    the future's marriage
to ancestral suffering.

No man can scale Schiehallion
                    by the handholds
of an other's grief
                    with ropes and footholds
of an other's pain

One human grief
                outweighs all promises.
Love is not measured
                and our only scale
                          is Jonathan's
slow music
        welling
                from the common deep
                            unique
through every individual.

The task
        impossible-continuous
                        to reconcile
the moon and sun
                insistent that today
                        larksong
come welling
            from the falcon's throat
that vinyards flourish
                olive trees bear heavy harvest
in each human heart
            to find
among the rubble
            of our failures
                disappointments
                griefs
in fissures
            of our faithlessness
                fear
                fickle pride
                    the unexpected blossomings
of love
        at its keenest
                not in a victory
                    but in defeat.

CONIVNCTIO SIVE
Coitus.

O Luna durch meyn vmbgeben/vnd suſſe mynne/
Wirſtu ſchön/ſtarck/vnd gewaltig als ich byn.
O Sol/ du biſt vber alle liecht zu erkennen/
So bedarffſtu doch mein als der han der hennen.

ARISLEVS IN VISIONE.

Coniunge ergo filium tuum Gabricum dile‐
ctiorem tibi in omnibus filijs tuis cum ſua ſorore
Beya

Only taking that impossible burden
on each individual back
                    can we hope to scale
Schiehallion's topmost pinnacle
                        to see the earth
go nova
          and outblaze the sun
                            in that reddest
dearest of all dawns.

Sweet prince, I shall not see that dawn
                            but must trek down
Schiehallion's other slope
                    into the broad strath of my days
and there
          from out my meadowed passions
                            loud with bees
salute the sun
            setting below heart's horizon
                            waiting
for my mistress of the star-pierced dark
                        to rise up in me
thirling me on threads of moonlight
                    onto white oblivion
her messenger
            the silver mare
              red-eyed and crazy
                        prancing from the moon
and band on circling band of agate
                    shattering
to rainbowed halos at my heart.

In partial light
          from this steep corrie
near to my summit
              not yet scaled
                        I see my homeland
spread below me

    in continuous kaleidescope
of anguished miracle.

Scotland
   ancient, raddled whore
       black devourer
festering through history
      where shall I find
that gay humility
    to kneel
      taste your mouth
bitter on my own
     until our kiss lets flow
some lambent wine?

Protean harlot
   I confess
     I have wasted whole days
in idleness
   enrapt before the shifting genius
        of your face
lain hours in your upwelling reverie
      of cloud, moor, dawn
have seen you sifting
    dreams of wind and wave
against the long sea-wall
     Scotland
      exhausting
      inexhaustible.

And in your generous, enfolding woods
       have heard you
faint among the leaves
    come whispering

   This too will pass.
   Bewilderment and pain
     will pass

and we be mingled once again
deep in our unmeasured wine.

and overhead
                    green banners of your passion
floating
        on the evening's breath
                                proclaiming
life
    through grief and death.

Scotland, if I knew how
                    I would make poems menacing
as Arab daggers
                hilts elaborately filigreed
and blades
            a naked radiance
                                to make your mouth go dry
and in this desert
                where the thistles flourish
would incise
            your crusted history
                                show you your cancers
until your tears and blood
                            congealing in our sullen waste
bore from this sand
                the fruits of Canaan
                                    Canaan of the desert
eagles
    and the songs.

Jonathan, the songs depart
                        the task remains
a man may not desist from
                        nor complete
                                    being
old bones in a leather bag

                    slick with faeces
                            blood, lymph, phlegm
griefs told in tears
and joys in semen
                water-music
                        of the body's well
having been
            a hare
                in hedgerows of desire
                                pursued
            a deer
                in thickets of despair
                                renewed.

I was a mute in Israel
                    a yellow star on my lapel.
I was a kiss
            in a city bar.
I was Skyhawk
            over Tyre
                    have drunk seed, whisky
                                gall and wine
philosophised and fantasised
                        betrayed, been loyal
after my fashion
                but from all these
                        have come to desire
only this
        from out the lucky-bag
                        of blood and dreams
to pluck some stone
                no emerald nor sapphire
but some fine, flawed piece
                    of red-veined quartz
may be unquarried at Schiehallion's core
or may be lies for all to see
                        in some high stream
above the moor

                    some token of my love
                                    for you.

Now let this love
                    discordant mover
be all
        my ritual
                    and ceremonial
incense and throbbing kettledrum.

Love is the key
                    to the seamless door
                                    no violence
may pry apart
                    love of the flesh
                                    the unembittered heart.

From desire
                to desire
                            to move and you, dark prince
to be my food
                    and I as hungry as the seed for light
                                    the lungs for air
                                    the mind for thought
sea for the moon
                    or time for man
                                    my fate to be
un-natural
            un-animal, un-god
                            in man, unmade
to be one breath of the struggle
            one tear of its anguish
                    star of its ecstasy
                                and in the love
of blond or black-haired
                        girl or boy
                                    be free to flow

                        79

through water-music to the sea
                              returning surf
against the cliffs
                of time and death, Tsvetayeva.

Among my listeners
                who hear
                        be true.
Retract no word
                no deed of love
                              in fear or need.
There is a loyalty of love
                        no claim of class
                                    nor state
                                    nor party
rightfully transcends.

Own no allegiance
                prior to that love.
Cherish no name
                nor soiled banner
                              and let not the name
of love
        shut out the light
                        love would create.

So to an ending
                an other beginning.
                              Those remain
who still ascend
                and I
                        who will not perpetrate this
                                                chase
on any child
                of body's seed
                              offer you, world, instead
my mad March songs.

May they wander among you
                    freely
                         may they waken love
in children
          of your children's seed.

So prince, my Jonathan
                    my poet-judge, my tawny seer
                    my netmaker to catch love in
I wait.

No cord ties down
               my mistress' image
                              on the stream
yet waxing and waning
                    it endures
                          so you abide
a cordless knot
          that may not be untied
demanding nothing
               and denying none
                         giving freely
ruling no-one
          seeking nothing
                    but to live and love.

Light sculpts the contours
                    of your mouth and cheeks
so into every lowly hollow
                    of the earth let's flow
together
          you and I
                    becoming like my friend the Samurai
could play
          cats at their own, sly games

whose muscular control
                                had come so near perfection
each response became
                        instinctual
                                yet conscious
as the cat's is not.

So consciousness in him
came near to turning
                        revolutionary
                                one full circle
                                of a sphere
                                without perimeter
a consciousness as simple
                playful
                graceful as a cat.

Teach me, Jonathan
                how to delight
                                neither to praise
                                nor to condemn
old, tarnished hearts
                or minds
                                perverted into vehemence
                        bodies
                                rigid as the stricken hare.

Let all my judgements of men be
                                provisional
equations in the languages
                        of love
                                a multilinear complexity
of passion on the lucid air.

Teach me to sway
                before the evening breeze
                                        and be not rigid
but erect

alert
      to play at being
            as a child swings
defying gravity.
Teach me
     at ending
        to be gay.

So though our home be bare
              of tapestry or frescoes
              of satyrs and temples
cellars be wine bereft
tables and boards bare
        still we are wine enough
          each for the other
        still we are warm enough
          twining together
and after gaiety
      to bed
        our bed of crazy creaking
               springs
mad burgeonings
     incongruous
        to waken into dreams
delicate eyelids
    offering
       to sleep
         blue-veined their marble
of the day's satieties.

hie ist geboren die eddele Keyserin reich/
Die meister nennen sie jhrer dochter gleich.
Die vermeret sich/gebiert kinder ohn zal/
Sein vnd ötlich rein/vnnd ohn alles mahl·

Die

Notes

Origen's remark is from *Homiliae in Leviticum* and the Marcuse and Gide quotations are from *One Dimensional Man* and *Later Fruits of the Earth* respectively.

Passionelle to Jonathan

passionelle	A litany of the sufferings of the Saints.
cité, cité	"Fourmillante cité, cité pleine de rêves", Baudelaire – first poet of the modern city.
diaspora	Originally the dispersion of the Jews among the Gentiles after the Babylonian Captivity and later, among the early Jewish Christians, the body of Jewish Christians outside Palestine. The Jew, the Gael, the Palestinian; a well-nigh universal phenomenon.
Jonathan	In *First Samuel* Jonathan is the friend, comrade and lover of David whom he protected from the jealous rages of King Saul, Jonathan's father. Jonathan was killed in battle with the Philistines from whose name derives the modern-day 'Palestine'.
white buck	A traditional Celtic image denoting among much else that rare and sacred creativity which is integrated with both a natural and a social order.

peacock	Was symbolic of immortality in medieval bestiaries.
vipers	The staff about which two vipers twine is the caduceus, carried by Hermes, patron of poets and gamblers. It is also carried by the Hermetic Hermes, Aesculapius and Serapis; all powers of healing and rebirth. The price of rebirth is death.
Bozez and Seneh	Are rocks named in *First Samuel*.
The Old King	Bres, High-King of Ireland, was obliged on account of his physical impurity, to relinquish the kingship. His affliction was the result of a nasty piece of satire directed against him by the poet Caibre.
Satanael	Was in Gnostic traditions Christ's dark, elder twin.
yew	Traditionally the death-tree of the Winter solstice.
Iain Lom	Was John MacDonald, Bard of Keppoch, the last great Clan poet and a staunch upholder of the traditional values of Gaeldom, chief among which were courage and loyalty. Directly involved in several political adventures, he was influential in his lifetime.
Owen Roe O'Neill	Of the family of Ulster warlords, a brilliant general, his early death lost to the cause of the Irish Gael a leader who might have held the Cromwellian tides at bay a little longer.
The Earls	Were O'Donnell and O'Neill who, with their retainers, fled Ireland in 1607.

Inverlochy	The battle in which, in 1645, Montrose hammered a largely Campbell army thanks to a timely warning from Iain Lom who watched the slaughter from a hillock and composed a poem in celebration of the event.
Montrose	Like Owen Roe, has become known as an upholder of the old order.
Limerick	Which sits on the Shannon estuary, was sacked by Cromwellian troops. There is a lovely air known in Scotland as *Lochaber No More* and in Ireland as the *Lamentations of Limerick*.
perch' io non spero	Is the opening line of a poem by Guido Cavalcanti, a friend of Dante.
silver cup	Is from Mackenzie's translation of *Fogradh Raghnaill Oig* (The Exile of Ranald Og) by Iain Lom – a token of past glories.
Mull	Once the island of the MacLeans and known now as The Officers' Mess on account of the number of retired Englishry buying land and houses at prices not to be afforded by the local people.
Sebastian	Saint and Roman soldier. Christian martyr, protector against pestilence. He was bound to a stake and shot with arrows, but surviving was beaten to death. The image fascinated a number of medieval artists. It is fundamentally an image of penetration like that of the Fisher King by the spear which pierced the side of Christ.
hawthorn	By the old calendar, the tree of the month

87

of enforced chastity, prelude to the excitements of Summer. Tree of my birthmonth.

Creation

Tsvetayeva

Marina Tsvetayeva was a Russian poetess who wrote a poem-sequence entitled *The Poem of the Mountain*. She hanged herself in 1941.

Ben Dorain

Is the title of Duncan Ban MacIntyre's most celebrated poem as well as a mountain by Glen Orchy.

Cuilin

Is the title of a poem by Sorley MacLean as well as a range of peaks on the Island of Skye.

Jehovah-Jireh

Is the peak on which Abram was to have sacrificed Isaac.

Phantoms & Skyhawks

American military aircraft used by the Israeli forces during the Six-Day-War.

Jerusalem Of Gold

During the Six-Day-War, the song *Jerusalem of Gold* swept Israel in a wave of nationalist sentiment. The refrain lines are; "Jerusalem of Gold, of Copper and of light, Indeed, I am a violin to all your songs."

stallion

At Ragnarok Odin will ride to battle against Fenris on a black stallion.

Karameh

"On 21st, March 1968 the battle of Karameh took place. A large Israeli column, led by tanks and with air support crossed the Jordan. The Palestinian commandos, who could have avoided combat, were ordered to stand

88

firm – and they held out for twelve hours. The Israeli troops suffered substantial losses, and a number of tanks were left behind on the battlefield . . . The Palestinian resistance organisations, acting in conscious violation of the laws of guerilla warfare, wanted to demonstrate that it was possible to stand up to the victors of the Six-Day-War without tanks and without aeroplanes.''; G. Chaliand, *The Palestinian Resistance*. (Penguin)

Loch nan Uamh	Means in Gaelic the Loch of the Caves. It is where Charles Edward landed in 1745 and whence he departed in 1746
Clan Donald	The Battle of Culloden, which broke feudalism in Scotland, saw the decimation of the Clan Donald contingents. Believing their honour to have been insulted by not having been given the Right of the Line, they refused to charge. Too proud and loyal to withdraw, they held their ground in the face of Butcher Cumberland's cannonade.
Cluny	Chief of Clan MacPherson.
Glenfinnan	Was where Charles Edward Stuart raised his standard.
John MacLean	Was a communist visionary whose work was mainly in Glasgow and on Clydeside. He stood out for a Scottish Worker's Republic, was imprisoned for his opposition to the great War and was appointed as a representative of the Soviet government by Lenin.

89

Raasay	The birthplace of Sorly MacLean.
Langholm	The birthplace of Christopher Grieve (Hugh MacDiarmid).
king	"When the King comes into his own again" was a phrase used by Jacobites in reference to the return of the exiled Stuarts.
silver mare	In the *Lailatal-Miraj*, or night-journey of Mohammed, the Prophet's dream of initiation into the mysteries of the cosmos began when the Archangel Gabriel approached, leading Elboraq, the half-human silver mare, who carred him in an instant to Jerusalem, the centre of the world.

Illustrations

The woodcuts were first printed in Frankfurt in 1550 in an anonymous tract entitled the *Rosarium Philosophorum;* a work describing the method by which base metals might be transmuted into gold. C. G. Jung has written at length on the psychological significance of the alchemists' writings and his essay *The Psychology of the Transference* is an exposition of the *Rosarium* woodcuts. According to Jung, the fantasy products embedded in the *Rosarium* chart a process of unselfconscious integration of conflicting psychic contents on the part of the author of the *Rosarium*. I have paraphrased freely.

Frontispiece	"We are the metal's origin and first nature, Through us the Art attains its final state. No water nor fountain is my peer I heal alike both rich and poor. My powers are both dangerous and great."

2
p. 16

"Mark well, in our Art nothing is concealed saving the central secret which may not be revealed to the uninitiated for to betray the secret would curse the traitor, bringing on him the wrath of God so that he would die in convulsions". The text goes on to say that errors in the Art arise from beginning with the wrong raw materials and that one must begin from what nature has given for only in and through nature is the Art generated and brought to completion.

3
p. 19

The King is saying; "O Moon, let me be your husband" and the Queen; "O Sun, I must submit to you". The dove carries the inscription; "The spirit gives life". The accompanying text specifies the qualities required of anyone who would undertake the Art.

4
p. 30

The water in which King and Queen are bathing is Mercurius, the alchemical spirit. The Philosopher's Stone which transmutes base metals into gold will be realised in the conjunction of perfect and imperfect bodies, spirit and flesh, I and thou.

5
p. 37

"Here the four elements divide as the soul from the corpse ascends".

6
p. 43

"Here King and Queen are lying dead In great distress the soul is fled".

7
p. 45

"Here is the soul descending to quicken the purified body".

8
p. 50

"Now King Sol is in eclipse beneath the spirit of Mercurious".

9
p. 70

"Here falls the heavenly dew, to lave the soiled body in the grave".

10
p. 74

"O Luna, held in my sweet embrace Be as strong as I, as fair of face. O Sol most radiant light known to men, Yet needing my light as the cock the hen".

11
p. 84

"Here the most noble Empress is born Whom the Philosophers call their daughter. She multiplies and bears many children Incorruptible and without stain".